FROM SEED TO SUNFLOWER

Anita Ganeri

Heinemann
LIBRARY

www.heinemann.co.uk/library
Visit our website to find out more information about Heinemann Library books.

To order:

 Phone 44 (0) 1865 888066

 Send a fax to 44 (0) 1865 314091

 Visit the Heinemann Bookshop at www.heinemann.co.uk/library to browse our catalogue and order online.

First published in Great Britain by Heinemann Library, Halley Court, Jordan Hill, Oxford OX2 8EJ, part of Harcourt Education. Heinemann is a registered trademark of Harcourt Education Ltd.

Editorial: Nancy Dickmann and Sarah Chappelow
Design: Ron Kamen and edesign
Picture Research: Ruth Blair and Kay Altwegg
Production: Helen McCreath

Originated by Modern Age
Printed and bound in China by South China Printing Company

ISBN 0 431 05074 0
10 09 08 07 06
10 9 8 7 6 5 4 3 2 1

The British Library Cataloguing in Publication Data
Ganeri, Anita
From seed to sunflower. - (How living things grow)
571.8'2399
A full catalogue record for this book is available from the British Library.

Acknowledgements
The Publishers would like to thank the following for permission to reproduce the following photographs:
Alamy pp. **5**, **9**, **10**, **12**, **14**, **15**, **16**, **17**, **18**, **20**, **21**, **23**, **24**, **25**, **27**, **29**; Ardea p. **19**; Corbis pp. **4**, **6** (Jim Sugar), **8** (Maurice Nimmo/Frank Lane Picture Agency); FLPA pp. **7** (Tony Hamblin), **22**, **26** (Wim Weenink/Foto Natura); Getty Images p. **13** (Photodisc); Science Photo Library p. **11** (Steve Taylor).

Cover photograph of a sunflower reproduced with permission of Nature Picture Library/Aflo.

Illustrations: Martin Sanders

Every effort has been made to contact copyright holders of any material reproduced in this book. Any omissions will be rectified in subsequent printings if notice is given to the publishers.

The paper used to print this book comes from sustainable resources.

Contents

Words written in bold, **like this**, are explained in the glossary.

Have you ever seen a sunflower?

A sunflower is a type of plant.
It has big, yellow flowers.
A sunflower
grows from a
large **seed**.

*Sunflowers can
grow very tall.*

You are going to learn about
a sunflower. You will learn how
a sunflower seed grows into a plant,
makes new seeds, and dies. This
is the sunflower's
life cycle.

Where does
a sunflower
seed grow?

5

Seeds in the soil

Sunflower **seeds** grow in the ground. In spring, people plant the seeds in the soil. They water the seeds to make them grow.

Some seeds are planted.

Some seeds are spread by birds.

Some seeds fall out of old sunflower plants. They stay in the ground over winter. Then they start to grow in spring.

How does the seed grow?

Growing seeds

The **seed** starts to grow in spring.
In each seed is a tiny new plant.
There is also a store of food for the
new plant to use.

*Sunflower seeds are protected by these
hard black and white seed cases.*

Sunflowers need water and sunlight all the way through their life cycle.

The way the seed starts to grow is called **germination**. The seed needs sunlight and water to make it grow.

Which part of the plant grows first?

First roots and shoots

After a few days, the first tiny **roots** start to grow. The roots push out of the **seed**. They grow down into the ground.

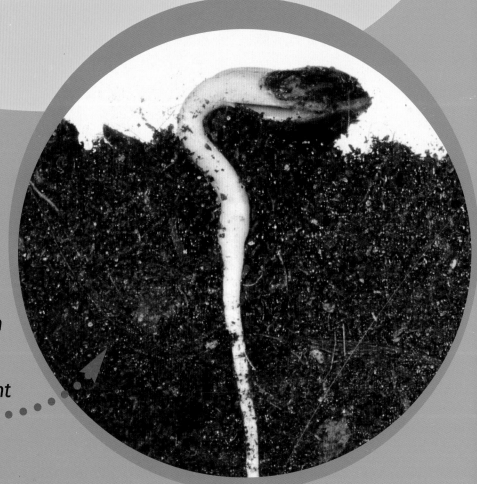

*The root soaks up water and **nutrients** from the soil. Roots also fix the plant in the ground.*

The shoot pushes the old seed shell out of the soil.

Next, a tiny green **shoot** grows from the seed. It pushes up through the soil into the light.

When do the leaves grow?

11

First leaves

After about a week, green leaves start to grow. They open out at the tip of the **shoot**. The leaves make food for the plant.

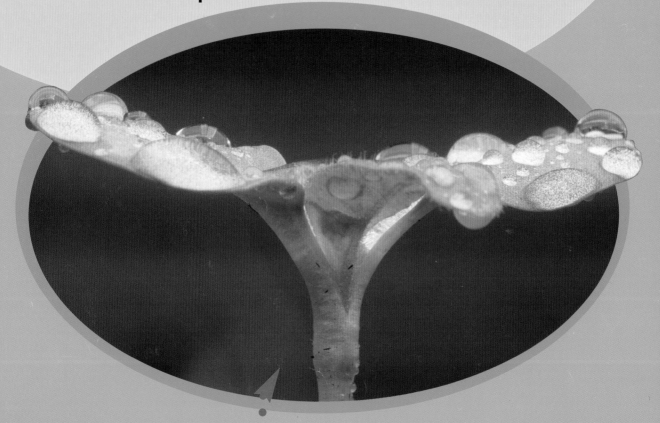

Like all living things, plants need food and water to live and grow.

The gas and water are turned into food in the leaves.

The leaves take in sunlight.

The leaves take in gas (**carbon dioxide**) from the air.

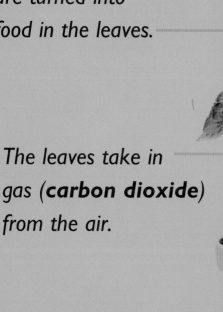

The **roots** suck up water from the soil.

This picture shows how a plant makes its own food. The way a plant makes its food is called **photosynthesis**.

What is the plant's **stem**?

13

Growing taller

The sunflower plant grows taller and taller. Its **shoot** grows stronger and straighter. The shoot is now called the plant's **stem**.

These sunflower plants may grow to be twice as tall as you!

Fine hairs on the stem stop insects climbing up and nibbling the plant.

The stem holds the plant up to the sunlight. The stem also moves food and water around the plant.

Where do the flowers grow?

Flower buds

The next part of the sunflower to grow is a big flower **bud**. This grows at the end of the **stem**. Leaf-like points called **bracts** grow around the bud.

The bracts protect the bud.

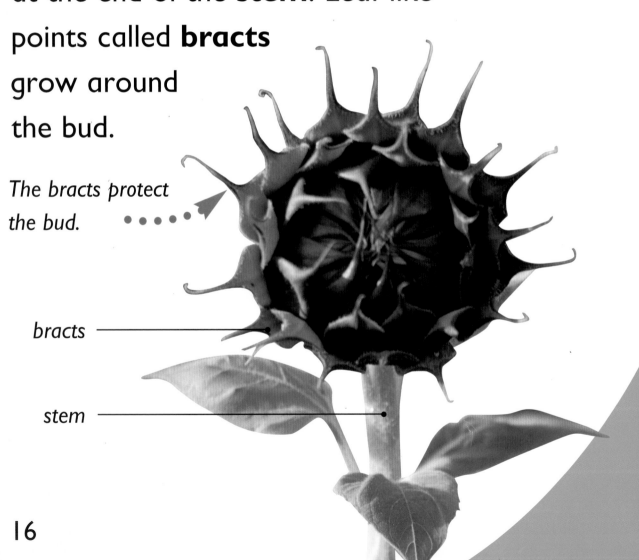

bracts

stem

The petals are starting to show.

Soon the bracts begin to unfold. The flower bud opens. In the ring of bracts there are lots of bright yellow petals.

What do flowers need to grow well?

17

Blooming flowers

It is now summer. The sunflowers are blooming. The flowers turn to face the sun. The plants need sunlight to help them grow.

The sun's heat and light help the flowers to grow.

A flower-head is about as big as a dinner plate.

Each flower is made up of lots of
tiny flowers. These tiny flowers are
called **florets**. The florets
grow in a big
group called a
flower-head.

Why do
bees visit
sunflowers?

19

Busy bees

Buzzing bees visit the sunflowers. The bees come to drink a sweet juice made by the flowers. The juice is called **nectar**.

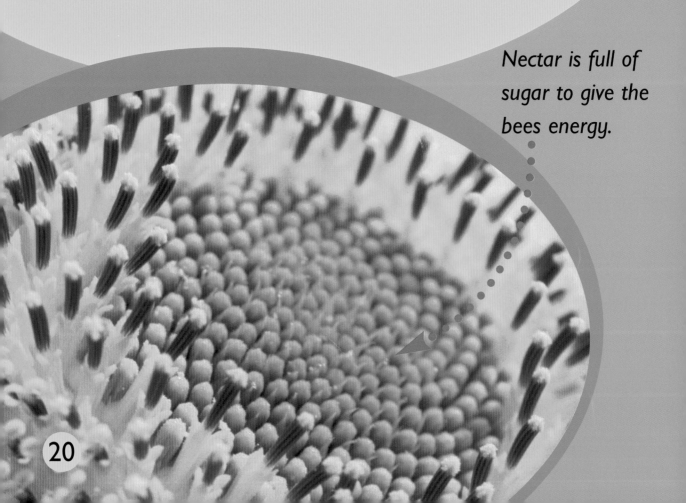

Nectar is full of sugar to give the bees energy.

The pollen sticks to the hairy bee as it drinks nectar.

The bees have to crawl across the **florets** to get to the nectar. The florets make a yellow dust called **pollen**.

What does the bee do with the pollen?

21

New sunflower seeds

The bee flies to another sunflower to drink its **nectar**. The **pollen** is still stuck to the bee. Some of the pollen rubs off the bee and on to the new **florets**.

pollen

Hundreds of seeds can grow on one flower-head.

The pollen joins with parts of the new florets. This is called **pollination**. Lots of new **seeds** start to grow on the **flower-head**.

What happens to the sunflower?

Dying sunflowers

The new sunflower **seeds** are growing so the flower has done its job. The petals droop and fall off. The flower dies.

The sunflower dies at the end of the summer.

People cut the dead plants down and save the seeds to use.

The **flower-head** is now a circle of black and white seeds. It gets so heavy with seeds that it droops from the end of the **stem**.

Who likes to eat the seeds?

25

Spreading seeds

Birds eat the **seeds** that people have not taken. The birds drop some of the seeds on the ground. These seeds may grow into new plants in the spring.

Each plant has made lots of new seeds.

Sunflower plants make one lot of flowers and seeds. Then the plants die in autumn or winter.

Life cycle of a sunflower

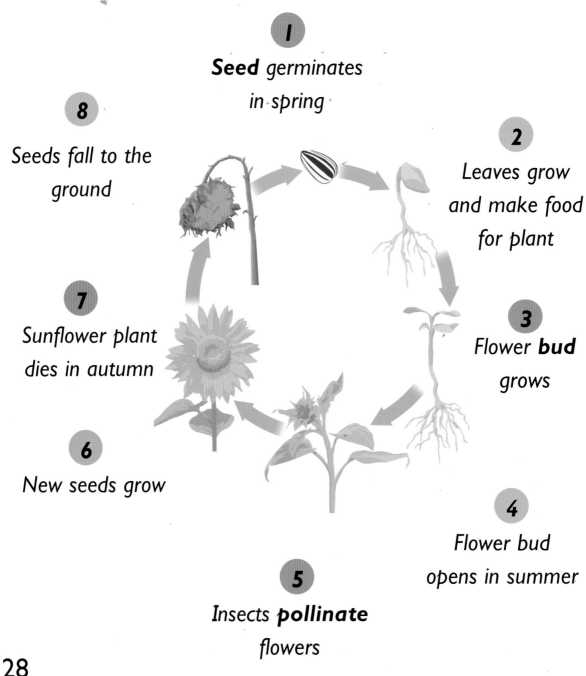

1
Seed germinates in spring

2
Leaves grow and make food for plant

3
Flower **bud** grows

4
Flower bud opens in summer

5
Insects **pollinate** flowers

6
New seeds grow

7
Sunflower plant dies in autumn

8
Seeds fall to the ground

Sunflower plant map

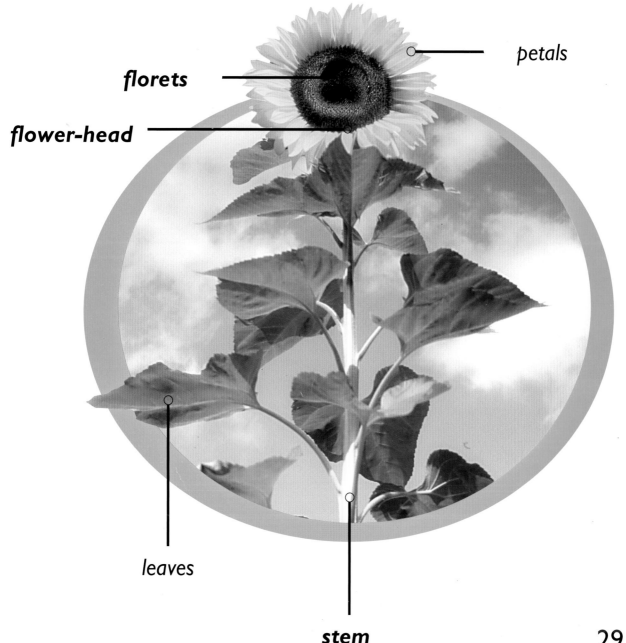

petals

florets

flower-head

leaves

stem

Glossary

bracts parts of a plant that protect the flower buds

bud the start of flowers or leaves

carbon dioxide gas in the air

florets tiny flowers which are part of a flower-head

flower-head large flower made up of lots of florets

germination how a seed starts to grow into a plant

nectar sweet juice made in a flower

nutrients food living things need to grow

photosynthesis how a plant makes its own food
from sunlight, gas, and water

pollen yellow dust made in a flower

pollinate take pollen from one flower to another

pollination how pollen joins with parts of a flower
to make new seeds

roots parts of a plant that grow into the ground

seed part of a plant that grows into a new plant

shoot new plant's first stem and leaves

stem plant's tall stalk

More books to read

Life as a Sunflower, Vic Parker (Heinemann Library, 2003)

Nature's Patterns: Plant Life Cycles, Anita Ganeri (Heinemann Library, 2005)

Websites to visit

Visit this website to find out more interesting facts about growing plants:

http://www.bbc.co.uk/schools/scienceclips

Disclaimer

All the internet addresses (URLs) given in this book were valid at the time of going to press. However, due to the dynamic nature of the internet, some addresses may have changed, or sites may have ceased to exist since publication. While the author and publishers regret any inconvenience this may cause readers, no responsibility for such changes can be accepted by either the author(s) or the publishers.

31

Index

Titles in the *How Living Things Grow* series include:

Hardback · · · · · · 0 431 05079 1

Hardback · · · · · · 0 431 05072 4

Hardback · · · · · · 0 431 05075 9

Hardback · · · · · · 0 431 05078 3

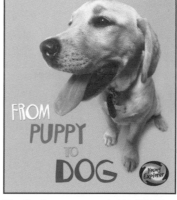

Hardback · · · · · · 0 431 05073 2

Hardback · · · · · · 0 431 05080 5

Hardback · · · · · · 0 431 05074 0

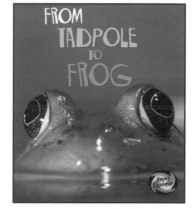

Hardback · · · · · · 0 431 05077 5

Find out about other Heinemann Library titles on our website www.heinemann.co.uk/library